LEADING WITH A SMILE

Be happy as a leader
and lead your people to happiness

Alex Slavenburg MiF MCM

Copyright © March 2021 by Alex Slavenburg.
All rights reserved.

Published by
Happimotion, Driebergen-Rijsenburg, The Netherlands
www.happimotion.com

For information or contact with the author:
info@happimotion.com

ISBN: 9798728842903

Book cover design by Dan Camacho
Original title: Leidinggeven met een glimlach (Dutch)
Translation by Copy Trust
Photo of Alex by Marcel Bosman

Contents

Foreword 4

Know thyself 7

Seek wisdom in silence 17

Do everything with intent and focus 27

Inspire and motivate others 37

Walk the talk 47

Encourage talent 55

Give people freedom 65

Never stop learning 75

Adopt a healthy lifestyle 83

Don't forget to smile 93

Checklist for leading with a smile 98

Reference list 100

Foreword

If you do a Google search on "*Leadership*" you'll find a few billion results and a search on Amazon.com gives you a list of over 60,000 books.

It is a popular topic which almost everyone has an opinion about. You also see this on LinkedIn, where posts and quotes about leadership appeal to a large audience and often go viral.

I have held a wide range of leadership positions, from branch manager to director, while working for Rabobank Group (an international bank in Food & Agribusiness) for more than two decades.

I have taken many courses and training programs and have read (and still read) a lot about leadership and in 2019 I decided to write a book myself.

Books on leadership describe a wide variety of styles, from servant leadership to situational leadership and from agile to feminine leadership.

But is it really that complicated? And has leadership really changed over the years or are employees' basic needs still the same?

The central premise of this book is: Wouldn't it be fantastic if managers could adopt "*leading with a smile*" as their preferred style?

What this means is that leadership becomes enjoyable, suits you, feels good and is appreciated by the people around you!

This book gives you practical tools that will help you, as a leading person, find that smile within you and bring a smile to the people you lead.

So, get inspired, dare to experiment and learn from new experiences.

Have fun reading!

Alex Slavenburg, March 2021

Chapter 1

Know thyself

> *"Getting in touch with your true self must be your first priority"*
> Tom Hopkins

Leadership. Everyone has an opinion about it, but what is it actually?

When you look up the word in the Merriam-Webster Dictionary, you'll see that the first definition of the term is **<u>leadership</u>**: 1. the office or position of a leader.

You'll often hear leadership defined as a "position," and therein lies the problem. A position of power is inherent in the definition—and therefore in everyday practice—which is essentially at odds with our need as humans for freedom and autonomy.

Did you know that managers are at least 70% responsible for the differences in employee engagement scores between departments? And that managers often have a negative effect on an organization's results? I also read in a survey that 25% of respondents cited the behavior of their manager as a reason for choosing another job.

In practice, I often see managers struggle with leadership tasks, not knowing what is expected of them and not being able to live up to expectations.

Leadership becomes a burden, and it is only after a lot of hardship that managers find out that leadership doesn't suit them.

*Leadership is an action,
not a position*

Leadership is something you can learn
This book is about leading with a smile and not "the position of the leader". Leadership is a skill and an activity that comes naturally to many people.

I'm not talking about the conventional view of a manager, which is "someone who manages and assesses a team at the end of the year". I like to think of it more broadly. Parents act as leader in their family, volunteers take on this role in associations, HR advisors in projects and, of course, managers in departments.

You often grow into the role of leader—you are asked to do it, or you take on the role because you have a lot of experience in a department and you become the head of that department organically.

The great thing to know is that leadership is a skill you can learn. And to find out what skills you already have and what skills you still have to learn, you have to start by discovering yourself.

Start with yourself
Your leadership has an impact on others. Managers often take on a leadership role without asking themselves if it suits them, and this can have far-reaching consequences.

The first step toward leadership is therefore to apply leadership principles to yourself. You have to know (or discover) yourself before you can lead others.

We call this Personal Leadership—getting the best out of yourself.

If you know yourself well and therefore know whether leadership suits you, you'll be able to shape the way you lead and consciously choose environments that suit your style of leadership.

Personality

Knowing yourself starts with understanding your personality. What is your personality and how has your upbringing shaped you?

A fantastic and scientifically well-founded tool to find out your personality type is the "Big Five" test, also known as the "OCEAN" test. Several sites offer this test online, which will give you a first impression of your personality within a few minutes.

Why is that important, you may ask. The five parts of the test give you a good idea of what you are capable of and where your strengths and natural abilities lie.

The table on the next page, where you can see if you have a High or Low score for each trait, gives a first impression of your own Big Five.

Usually there are two or three areas you strongly identify with-in the description Low or High.

If you identify somewhat with both traits in an area, gives you an "average" score.

Low	Personality Traits	High
Preserver Practical, efficient, present	Originality	**Explorer** Curious, creative, future
Flexible Spontaneous, playful, embraces chaos	Consolidation	**Focused** Organized, planner, perfectionist
Introvert Reserved, calm, independent, quiet	Extroversion	**Extrovert** Gregarious, talkative, friendly, energetic
Challenger Competitive, critical, seeks own limits	Agreeableness	**Collaborator** Team player, helpful, seeks harmony
Resilient Calm, rational, low stress	**Need for stability**	**Responsive** Alert, tense, emotions

Knowing your Big Five profile is the first step to taking your personality into account when it comes to leadership.

Does the test show that you score low on extroversion and high on task orientation, but your role requires you to give a lot of presentations to large groups? Then you'll recognize that giving these presentations often costs a lot of energy.

The outcome of the test will give you a rough idea of what your aptitude is and can point you in the direction of what kind of role suits you.

A score is never right or wrong—it gives you an idea of your personality type and therefore helps you to develop and perform your role more effectively.

If you would like to know more about this, I highly recommend "For Personality at Work," a book by Pierce J. Howard with leadership tips for each type. "Happiness at Work" by Onno Hamburger and Ad Bergsma is another insightful book that describes the relationships between the Big Five and Happiness at Work.

A compass gives you your bearings and directions

What's your compass?
Another way to get to know yourself better and therefore cultivate your personal leadership style is to discover your inner compass.

This compass consists of three elements—your values, your motives, and your strengths and qualities.

Here too, you can draw up your own list based on various tests.

Obviously, the best way is to consciously reflect on these three elements first and ask co-workers or friends how they perceive you in this respect.

To get started, you can consider the following questions.

Values	• What is important to you? • What is your sense of purpose? • Who do you admire? • What do you truly dislike? • What do friends, your boss, others say about you?
Motives	• What makes you tick? • What gives you energy? • When do you get into a state of flow? • When do you get satisfaction in your work?
Qualities	• What comes easily to you? • What do people appreciate about you? • Which of your skills do people often call upon? • What were you good at as a child?

Once you have a good grasp of these three elements, choose up to five outcomes for each. Together, these form your compass in your work and your leadership style. This compass gives you a good idea of what kind of leader you are, what motivates you, and what your distinctive qualities are.

My compass, for example, is as follows:

Values	Drivers	Qualities
1. Autonomy	1. Meet People	1. Love
2. Health	2. Connecting	2. Leadership
3. Gratitude	3. Gaining confidence	3. Friendly & Generous
4. Uniqueness	4. Create motion	4. Fair & Honest
5. Flow	5. Get results	5. Optimism

Ask for feedback

Feedback is a valuable tool in getting to know yourself and finding out how others see you. Giving feedback is often a delicate matter. We find it unnerving and it often leads to more problems because we're not good at giving feedback without making judgments and/or telling the other what our own feeling is.

But asking for feedback is quite different. Try the following to see what happens.

Exercise:
- Find *a co-worker* you work with often.
- Go for a *walk* together (a Zoom or teams meeting works as well).
- First ask *"What do you appreciate about how we work together?"*
- Then ask *"And what do you sometimes find difficult?"*
- As the inquiring party, you should only ask *insightful questions*.
- After that, all you have to say is *"thank you"*.
- What you could also do is *switch roles in the conversation* and do the exercise again.

I often see, by doing such exercises, that people start to appreciate each other more—and therefore express this more—and are able to discuss sore points more easily.

This can lead to great conversations, and even when you have been working together for many years it can reveal surprising things about each other.

I can already hear you think "Phew... I don't have time for that, I'm busy and I have so many other things to do!" But be assured that getting to grips with what I have outlined above will help you and your team. The next chapter will give you the tools you need to hone your leadership skills.

Chapter 2

Seek wisdom in silence

> *"The best thinking has been done in solitude.*
> *The worst has been done in turmoil"*
> Thomas A. Edison

BUSY! This is probably the most-heard answer when you ask someone "How are you?". Being busy is true for a lot of people and especially for managers. And they are often very busy—coming up with plans, implementing plans, meeting expectations, doing their work.

They often have to attend a raft of (online) meetings with no breaks in between, and that's a pity. In her book *"Top Five Regrets of the Dying,"* Bronnie Ware describes the five regrets people speak about in their dying moments, some of which will be familiar to many of us:

- "I wish I hadn't worked so much".
- "I wish I'd the courage to live a life true to myself, not the life others expected of me".

I'd like to take you through some of the possible causes and consequences and, of course, offer a few solutions.

BUSY BUSY BUSY is a mantra we often hear, and it prevents us from taking the time to reflect on things that matter, including ourselves (as I talked about in Chapter 1). So, what is keeping us all busy and is this something new?

Tony Crabbe gives us an answer to this in his book *"Busy: How to Thrive in a World of Too Much"*.

Among the reasons he gives for us being constantly busy are the following:

1. *Being busy is easier*: it is easier to stay busy than make tough decisions. When we're constantly busy, we often react to things rather than consciously choose our actions.

2. *Being busy is avoidance*: often the things you resolve to do are not the easiest (such as exercising more, thinking about your future, working less hard) and we tend to postpone these difficult kinds of things.

3. *Being busy is a brand*: in other words, being busy lends us a status which many people around us have as well. Just say "I'm relaxed" when someone asks, "How are you?" and you already find yourself formulating a more defensive answer.

4. *Being busy is addictive*: today's social media—with the famous tiny red dots, email checking, and abundance of information on the internet—constantly draw us in and give us stimulating dopamine hits. Our brain always wants more and being busy delivers just that.

Is this new? Yes and no.

Studies into how people spend their time show that the number of annual hours worked in the U.S. in 1979 averaged 1,817 hours and in 2017 it was 1,757 hours, or 3.3% less. Those work hours make up "only" 20% of our total time (of 8,760 hours per year). Not too bad, right?

Choice stress
It would appear that our busyness is mainly in our perception. This is evident from the amount of information we're exposed to, for example.

Since the 1980s, this amount has increased by a factor of two hundred whereas our brain is now used to processing "only" five times as much information.

It means we're living in a world of information abundance, which all too often leads to FOMO, Fear of Missing Out.

This fear is partly rooted in the fact that abundance forces us to do something we're not particularly good at: choosing.

Many of our decisions are based on "yes or no" choices and too often the answer is "yes," which makes us even busier. New project? Yes! Could you help me with it? Yes!

What we should be doing is making more "which" choices, says Crabbe.

This allows you to make conscious choices and to say no to things more often, thus reducing busyness.

Our brain is always switched on, always under pressure and almost always sending us signals!

This means that our brain is less capable of making difficult choices and therefore less capable of deciding what we will (and especially will not) do. Saying no is therefore incredibly difficult.

Avoiding stillness
In fact, it is even worse... As humans, we find stimuli particularly pleasurable. A 2014 study in the journal *Science* found that 67% of men and 25% of women would rather give themselves a painful electric shock than spend 15 minutes alone in a room with nothing to do. Avoiding stillness is evidently worth a lot.

This brings us to some promised tools that can help reduce the pressure we experience.

> *Stillness gives your brain downtime*
> *and allows it to grow.*
> *Your mind becomes less busy and chaotic*

From now on, don't use the word "busy"
In 2011, I spoke with my management team about the results of the employee survey, which showed poor scores for Workload in particular.

One of the agreements we made was to stop using the word "busy". I haven't done so since, and this was particularly hard in the beginning because you almost automatically say "busy!" when someone asks, "How are you?" or "How was your day?" Even worse is "How are you? Busy, I guess?!"

By persevering and not using the word "busy" anymore, you bring awareness to the process and start using different language.

So now that we're on the right track, I'd like to give you a few more tips on how to break the Busy Chain".

Read the book "*How to Break Up with your Phone*"
This is an accessible and insightful book by Catherine Price about how to have a healthy relationship with your smartphone. Since their advent in 2007, smartphones have become a ubiquitous part of our streetscape.

At the same time, they are our #1 source of stimulation and cause a lot of frustration. Use the tips in this book to establish a fresh, new, and healthy relationship with your smartphone in thirty days!

Take time to reflect
Another thing you can do is take time to reflect on past situations and choices.

Before you know it, your calendar is fully booked for the next five weeks, so you need to make time to "catch your breath" and do something else instead of being in "busy mode" as usual.

You can start by setting aside 15 minutes every day at the end of the day (or before you go to sleep if necessary ☺) to ask yourself a few questions:

- What went well today?
- What am I grateful for today?

And some bonus questions:

- What should I perhaps not have done?
- What would I have liked to do differently?
- What do I plan to do tomorrow?

> *Our subconscious mind has a processing capacity 200,000 times greater than our conscious mind*

Meditate
There's an interesting book by Dutch author Ap Dijksterhuis about "the power of your subconscious". His message is that you cannot "control your mind" just by thinking and being conscious of things. Your subconscious is extremely powerful and largely determines your actions, so it would be a pity not to make use of it.

One tried and tested way to engage your subconscious is through *meditation*. By seeking stillness, you can discover your own wisdom.

Learning to meditate is a matter of practice. Here are three examples to inspire you:

1. *10 x 1 to 10 x 30*

My first introduction to meditation was through my coach during the time I was working in California. I was living in my head a lot, thinking about my future and feeling restless. He suggested I do the following exercise:

Sit upright on the floor, set a timer for 10 minutes, count from 1 to 10 and focus on your breathing. Repeat this until the timer goes off. Do this every day for at least 30 days.

You'll notice (as I did) that thoughts come and go, like clouds, and that you'll usually feel calm after the meditation and new ideas or images will arise from your subconscious.

2. *Calm, Breethe, Headspace*

There are also many apps that can help you meditate. One of my favorites is Breethe, with a lot of different exercises. The apps give you instructions, often with soothing background music and a calming voice, that help you to make meditation a habit.

With that you actually get real benefit from your smartphone for at least ten minutes a day.

3. *Doing nothing*

Time Magazine recently devoted a great article to *Niksen*, the Dutch art of doing nothing, which has been touted as the latest stress-busting tool. "Doing nothing" is nothing new of course, but it is something I highly recommend you try.

Plan an hour or afternoon of doing nothing, walking around aimlessly, hanging out on the sofa, and relaxing without doing anything.

Good to know: scientific research has shown that stillness reduces stress and tension and renews brain cells.

Last but not least

Although these tips may seem impractical or even far from your mind, my advice is to try them anyway. Give them a shot and see what works best for you. Remember the Regrets of the Dying...

And, just to be clear, busyness is not inherently bad! Enjoying what you are doing, being productive and creative, with just the right amount of stress, is amazing! And, as with everything else, do it with focus!

Chapter 3

Do everything with intent and focus

> *"We are the generation capable of doing many things at once, without enjoying any of them"*
> Dinesh Kumar Biran

As the quote suggests, we do many things every day, often at the same time, without consciously enjoying them. We engage in multitasking, only to discover that we're not that good at it.

We find it hard to truly focus on things and there are many distractions and temptations, such as email, smartphone, social media, chatting with co-workers in the office garden, and so on.

So, in this chapter I'd like to focus on the power of intent—how do you do that? And how does your intent and focus influence others?

Try the Pomodoro Technique
There's an extremely handy tool to help you focus and stop you from constantly turning your attention to distractions. This technique, developed by Francesco Cirillo in the late 1980s during the advent of email, is often mentioned in time management books.

Now, as you may know, you cannot manage time—we all have precisely 168 hours a week—but you can practice how not to give in to all those distractions.

How does it work?

First, buy a kitchen timer and if you want to do it like Francesco, get one in the shape of a pomodoro: a tomato. If that's too old-school for you, search "tomato timer" on Google for an online timer.

Using your tomato timer (or your digital timer), you can train yourself to work on a task with full concentration for 25 minutes, after which you give yourself a short break.

THE POMODORO TECHNIQUE

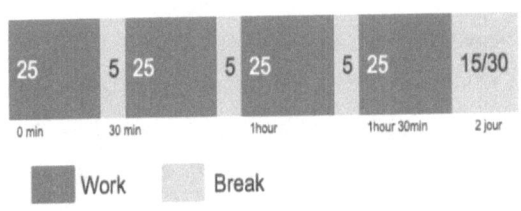

Exercise:
There are five steps in the Pomodoro Technique:
1. Decide which task you are going to tackle. What's your goal?
2. Close your email program and mute your phone.
3. Set the timer for 25 minutes and work towards your goal until the timer goes off.
4. Take a short break (5 minutes).
5. Take a longer break (15 to 30 minutes) after every fourth "Pomodoro".

Just try it and see how hard it is to sustain. It really helped me a lot when I was writing this book.

Practice makes perfect, of course, and it changes the way you work so that you can truly focus on a task and make progress. An additional benefit is that in those 25 minutes you can enter a state of flow, which I'll talk about more in Chapter 6.

Multitasking has an adverse effect on relationships

When asked about multitasking, people often say "Sure, I know how to multitask". How often do you find that a manager says he or she is really listening during a meeting but is actually doing all sorts of things on their phone or laptop?

Should they not do this? Well, it depends on the perception of the person experiencing this. But the effect is usually not positive—after all, it is about the relationships between people. How many times have you sat in a meeting and noticed attendees multitasking? And how often did anyone say something about it?

I was guilty of it too, until one of my employees gave me direct feedback and told me how it affected her. She did that wonderfully and it has had a lasting effect on my behavior. Nowadays, I just say I cannot multitask, what a relieve!

Unfortunately, this (her calling me out on my behavior) is an exception. Often nothing is said, and this does affect the relationship, either consciously or unconsciously. Others start to doubt whether you are really listening.

This is not surprising, given that a survey in 2019 found that one of the most frequently listed criticisms about managers, both by men and women, was "My manager doesn't listen properly".

Listening = Attention = Connection
Not listening properly can have various causes, such as doing most of the talking yourself, doing two things at once, pretending to listen while thinking about what you are going to say next or thinking about other things.

So, it is good to know that employees really appreciate it when they are listened to; they notice it! Being able to listen is therefore an important leadership trait, and this requires establishing a basis of trust (see more on this in Chapter 4).

The 4 "A"s
As a manager, you can learn how to improve your listening skills and pay more attention to others by applying the following "A"s when talking to people:

1. <u>Accepting without judging</u>
   This doesn't mean you have to agree with what the other person is saying or that your judgment is wrong. However, you can consciously put your opinion aside and engage in a conversation with the other person.

   Often this is the hardest of the "A"s for managers, as we all judge in a split second; it is just in our nature to do that!

   The art is to suspend your internal judgment ("why are you so upset", "don't be silly", "I'll take care of it myself", and so on) when someone tells you something in a conversation and to remain curious.

2. <u>Ask questions, summarize and listen</u>
   If you can manage to accept without judging, you'll also be able to truly connect with the other person. You do this by being responsive to what you hear, see, and feel during the conversation. The familiar technique of listening, summarizing, and asking questions still works, but we just don't do it enough.

   How often have you heard co-workers start talking about their own experiences when you say during a break "I'm going on a trip to San Diego".

Chances are someone will say "That's nice, I went there five years ago," or "I'm going to Santa Monica soon," and so on.

Do you do that too? My tip: Try to ask three open-ended questions when someone says something before you start talking about yourself. I still find it a fun exercise and it always works! This way you bring more layers to the conversation. It also helps to be curious and creative when asking questions. Not only does the other person feels heard and seen, but it also gives you a lot of information you might otherwise have missed.

> *One of the greatest compliments you can give someone is to give them your full attention.*

3. <u>**A**ttention, being fully present</u>
   To have a good conversation, you have to give the other person your undivided attention—being present in the moment rather than preoccupied with other things. If you notice this is the case, first let them know or note it down somewhere and only then engage in a conversation. In other words, allow for a reset. This way the other person will see that you are interested and willing to take time for them.

4. <u>Authenticity, be yourself</u>
   The fourth A is perhaps the most important—be yourself and be authentic in everything you do! As a trainer, I often notice trainees struggle a bit with this. "Is this really my style, I'm quite direct, I just say what I think," and so on.

   The point is not to put on a show and pretend to be present, as the other person will immediately sense this. Develop your conversational repertoire based on the 4 "A"s, start practicing them and make them your own in a way that works for you. You'll start to regularly discern a smile toward the end of a conversation. ☺

Use all your senses
One last but crucial element of leadership with intent and focus is to engage all your senses. Use them in conversations with others.

We often put a lot of emphasis on "What do I hear?" but you can also learn a lot from with "What do I see?" by paying attention to body language, emotions, and behavior. "What do I feel?" is a question that can serve as an internal mirror but also to identify what you sense in the other person, such as tension, pleasure, fear, or anger.

By being aware of your observations and drawing on them during conversations you get a greater understanding of the other person but also demonstrate that you are paying attention to them. In turn, this helps them articulate their own emotions.

This allows you to truly connect and that is the very thing you need to be able to inspire and motivate others. So let's discover that in the next chapter!

Chapter 4

Inspire and motivate others

"There are only two ways to influence human behavior: you can manipulate it, or you can inspire it"
Simon Sinek

The first three chapters have given you a solid foundation from which to grow: getting to know yourself; have an inner compass; you know how to deal with pressure; what the power of stillness is; and thanks to the tips in Chapter 3, you work with greater focus and attention.

Time for the next step!

As said earlier, Leadership is not a position but an action, and this action primarily impacts others. Your leadership influences others and if you do this consciously, it often leads to great results. People are more likely to be inspired if they understand "the Why". So in a leadership role, you should be able to bring across the story and motivate people.

Start with Why!
One of the ways in which you build your role as a leader is by clearly communicating a vision, and to illustrate this I'd like to briefly mention Simon Sinek.

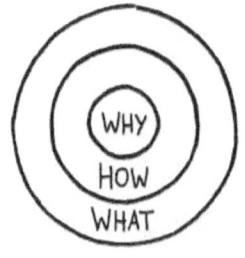

During his TEDx Talk "Start with why, how great leaders inspire action" in 2009, Sinek drew the golden circle with which he explains the How, What and Why. Since then, his TEDx Talk has been viewed millions of times on YouTube. Sinek contends that most companies (and leaders) mostly talk about the How and the What.

His message is to start with the Why of you and your organization—what is the goal of your project, what is your purpose as an organization? Taking that story as the foundation, you'll be able to inspire others in a way that is powerful and successful.

What is the Why with which your department or organization can inspire others?

Inspire? Be inspired!

Can you learn how to inspire others?
That's a good question! It is partly about your aptitude for conveying a story, connecting with people and being able to empathize with others. But the key to success is whether you yourself are inspired.

Lance Secretan, former director of Manpower, has written several books, including *"Inspire!"* and *"What Great Leaders Do!"*. He uses the metaphor of (among others) a spark and a flame to describe how to inspire others.

Spark
We can't give what we don't have! Are you inspired? What is your spark that lights the flame?

Flame
Your spark inspires others, and this ignites a flame within the organization.

So, the fundamental question is: what inspires you as a leader? What gives you energy? What is it you can't stop talking about?

If these are the things you want to achieve as an organization or a project team and which you therefore want to convey to others in your role as a leader, inspiring others will come almost naturally.

And while there is a clear distinction between inspiring and motivating, both of them are essential!

Of course, it is great if people are naturally motivated to engage in activities. However, a manager also has an important role to play in this process.

We distinguish between motivating and inspiring as follows:

Motivate	Inspire
Nudging people	Pulling people
Doing things the right way	Doing the right things
Completing an assignment	Communicating a vision
Works in the short term	Works continuously
Stoking a fire	Sparking an internal flame

Motivating is often viewed as negative and pushy, but I have found that giving attention to and motivating employees really helps. The key is to strike a good balance and make sure it is not just about motivating others, because then you run the risk of smothering personal initiative.

Three leadership hats
Inspiring and motivating are both important characteristics of leadership. As a leader, especially one who is also "hierarchically" responsible for employees, you have three roles, which I like to think of as three hats.

The three hats of leadership

Leader
As a leader, you inspire people with your story and communicate the mission, vision, and strategy of the organization. You know your organization's values and demonstrate these in action.

You also use these values to connect and energize your employees. Storytelling can help you get your message across more effectively. And the best stories are those that are passed on.

Manager
As a manager, you translate your vision into goals and are committed to monitoring and achieving these goals. You motivate your team, focus on output, make adjustments, intervene where necessary and take on a coordinating role when problems arise. Traditionally, the manager was often the one who solved all the problems, partly because he or she knew the most about what was going on. Fortunately, I see this less and less in organizations.

Coach
The third leadership hat is that of a coach. You encourage others to come up with their own solutions, you give them your attention, and you trust your people. You are honest and direct, give feedback as needed and help the other person develop.

In your leadership role, you have three hats, each of which represents a role. It is helpful to be aware of this so that you can decide which hat (role) is best suited to the goal you wish to achieve.

Fourth hat
Incidentally, leaders often have a fourth hat—that of an expert. Take, for example, an assistant foreman or a director of an accountancy firm who also has his or her own clients. This fourth hat often puts a strain on leadership and you have to make choices, especially in terms of what you want to focus on.

> *Motivated people are more likely to live up to their potential than unmotivated people*

How do you motivate people?
Motivation is often what you do when wearing your manager's hat. It can be quite hard to motivate others; managers may focus primarily on what is not going well. Sometimes, due to lack of time, they pay no attention at all to employees. Luckily, by now you'll have read some tips on how to avoid this.

The question is, how do you motivate people? It requires focus and attention, and there are a number of basic things you can do to accomplish this.

1. **Empathy.** Empathize with the other person. You can use the 4 "A"s in Chapter 3 to help you with this. Be aware of what is going on, be curious about the other person's motives, work with them on their strengths, show interest, and build a relationship.

2. **Be alert!** Be alert to what is happening, walk around the department, observe, and stay abreast of what is going on. Share what you see and hear with your people so that they sense your alertness and can contribute to it.

3. **Ask questions.** Again, ask open questions, do not judge too quickly, remain curious, and show understanding for the other person, even if you do not share their opinion.

Appreciation greatly enhances people's happiness at work

Appreciation and giving compliments are two particularly important aspects of motivation. Studies show that among employees who highly score the question "How happy are you at work?" there is a high correlation with the question "How much appreciation do you get from your manager?"

People who receive "a lot of" appreciation give a high score for happiness at work (around 8 on average), while those who receive "little" appreciation give an average score of around 6. Appreciation is therefore essential and affects aspects like "enjoyment at work," "good atmosphere," "trust in management," and "able to be myself".

The Languages of Appreciation

Appreciation is more than giving compliments.

In their book *"The 5 Languages of Appreciation in the Workplace,"* Gary Chapman and Paul White describe five recognizable ways to give appreciation. As a manager, it is extremely helpful to know the differences between and especially to discover the preferences of each employee. This is something you can quickly pick up. The five languages of appreciation are:

- **Words of affirmation:** written or expressed verbally, for a person or a group
- **Quality time:** by spending time with each other, being able to talk about what's on your mind
- **Acts of Service:** helping with the work, getting a task done together
- **Tangible Gifts:** a cup of coffee, a meal, a gift voucher etc.
- **Physical touch:** giving a high five, a fist bump or a hand on the shoulder.

Giving appreciation motivates people and makes them happy. As you can see, there are many ways in which you can show your appreciation.

Which ones do you prefer, and which ones do your people prefer? A great tip, and a fun way to find out during a team meeting, is that people often express their appreciation in a way that most appeals to them.

So, if you regularly get a gift from someone, they will most likely appreciate getting one from you.

Chapter 5

Walk the talk

"Example is not the main thing in influencing others. It is the only thing".
Albert Schweitzer

Your behavior under a magnifying glass

You often hear it at staff parties, at lunch or during meetings—people describing the behavior of a manager along the lines of "Did you see that?" or "You'll never guess what I saw John do yesterday".

As a manager, you operate under a magnifying glass and it seems like everyone has an opinion about your behavior. Employees will first take a wait-and-see approach, assess how you are doing, and then decide whether or not they actually want to follow you.

How you take the lead is a measure of how your entire team operates. One great example I recall is the introduction of a new CRM system. During a staff meeting, the managers talked about the importance of a good CRM system and its value for outstanding customer service.

When employees later discovered that the managers themselves did not make time to record their own interactions with customers in the CRM system, you can guess what the outcome was. Just as good examples are contagious, so are bad ones.

As a leader, you have to set an example—you have to walk the talk.

In other words, your behavior and everyday actions must be authentic and correspond to the organization's values, standards, and aspirations. Exuding confidence in your mission, being clear about your expectations, and taking the lead are essential.

Authenticity
Authenticity is about "being real". If you know yourself well (Chapter 1), it is much easier to do what you say. Be true to yourself and don't try to feign authenticity because employees can see through that. Being yourself can make you feel vulnerable at times, but in the long run, it is the most sustainable way to lead. Authenticity creates trust and keeps the connection strong, and employees sense and appreciate that authenticity.

Pointing out visible behavior leads to real change

Walk the talk
Drawing on my own experiences, I have listed a couple of tips that can help you, as a leader, make "walk the talk" work for you in practice:

1. Work on building shared core values and beliefs with your team.
2. Then make sure the choices you make (policy/vision/strategy/ideas) are consistent with these core values and beliefs.
3. Clarify exactly what needs to change in the organization or your department and set clear goals.
4. Determine the change through visible behavior, which is behavior you can see, demonstrate, and emulate.
5. Communicate these goals and behaviors clearly within your organization/team.
6. Set a good example yourself, be consistent and predictable.

This should especially translate to your behavior as a leader. If, for instance, you believe that "attention for each other" is important but are always in meetings yourself and hardly make time for your people, it will be counter-productive to what you want to achieve.

I recently heard an employee say, "My supervisor always says, 'my door is always open,' but he's never there". Time for a good talk, then!

The more you do what you say is important, the more credible you are. And as the saying goes, trust comes on foot (so you have to do your best) and leaves on horseback (one insincere step and people quickly jump to conclusions).

It is actually not that hard. Below are a few examples of "attention for each other" translated into what I like to call "visible behavior". It is behavior you can see, demonstrate, and emulate.

Block your calendar
This is something I have done myself for many years and it really works! Block one hour twice a day in your calendar. During those hours, don't schedule anything, walk around the department, call people or surprise employees who have asked for a moment of your time. Of course sometimes you have to schedule an activity in the timeslot you have blocked, but often you still have some time left to walk around and connect with co-workers.

Hello!
How often do you walk around the department or get into the elevator without saying "hello" or "good morning?" Sadly, in practice, I see at many companies that people just walk past each other without saying a word. It is the same thing in the elevator—most people will be absorbed in their smartphones.

Try to make it a habit to say "hi" or ask someone in the elevator "anything awesome happen today?"

You'll be surprised by the effect! And... good examples are contagious.

"Hanging around at reception"
Another example is a client advisor who worked at a bank that greatly valued customer focus. There were all kinds of rumors about him in infamous corridors, as he was always "hanging around at reception". Shouldn't he be working?

Until someone asked him what he was doing. It turned out he always went to the reception three minutes before a client arrived. Clients were always delighted; for once they didn't have to wait ten minutes for the advisor to come down. He took customer experience as the starting point and translated this into visible behavior.

Minus 40 degrees
My last example is a manager within a large technical company where teamwork is considered an important value in the corporate culture. The employees work in 24/7 shifts and in cold storages with temperatures of -40°. The manager schedules room in his calendar to work a half-day shift at least once a month. It's a bit like the principle behind the TV show *"Undercover Boss,"* only in this case it is not undercover. It is a perfect way to feel part of the team, stay connected to the

practical side of things, and pay attention to your people.

Exemplary behavior
At the end of the day, it is all about exemplary behavior. As a leader, you are always in the spotlight and others are always paying close attention to what you are doing.

There are plenty of occasions to lead by example.

If you think it is important for everyone to be on time at a meeting, be on time yourself.

If certification and e-learning is an important part of your strategy, make sure you yourself are always up-to-date and make time to complete e-learnings.

The same goes for utilizing development budgets. A growing number of organizations have agreements in their CLA (Collective Labour Agreement) concerning sustainable employability, or to put it more clearly: "How do I stay happy and successful at work until my retirement?"

It turns out there are many companies where 50 to 60% of the development budget is not used—including managers and executives. This sets a bad example, especially given the importance of developing talent, which I'll discuss in the next chapter.

Chapter 6

Encourage talent

> *"To get a grape and a talent to maturity requires rainy but also sunny days"*
> Friedrich Nietzsche

I regularly have discussions about Talent Development—whether or not to have separate classes, how much should you invest in employees, should you cut budgets when things are down and even if you should invest at all, because what if they leave?

Encouraging talent is one of the most important prerequisites for leading with a smile. My premise is "everyone has talent", a wonderful starting point for you as a manager, do you feel the energy?

One of the foundations of talent development can be found in positive psychology, a movement that emerged at the end of the 20th century and that focuses on the question "When do people do well?".

Positive psychology is a school of thought that sits alongside more traditional psychology, which focuses mainly on where things go wrong with people (like burn-out, illness, etc.).

> *The grass is greener where you water it*

Mastery
Managers tend by nature to focus mainly on the negative things—what is not working, what is not going well—and hold people to account on this.

Often they will resort to a directive style of leadership, with behavior like coordinating, monitoring, controlling, or sometimes even taking over and doing it yourself.

Especially when things get tense, managers tend to "manage" even more, yet it is precisely then that giving people freedom and trust helps them to truly develop their talents.

As a leader, it is important to get the best out of yourself and especially to let others flourish. Everyone is unique and has their own qualities and talents. The art is to mine this talent and encourage people to discover and use their talents.

This is also evident from research by Dan Pink, who describes the three essential elements that intrinsically motivate people in his book *"Drive"*.

Purpose	A meaningful goal gives people a reason to come to work (see Chapter 4 on "The Why").
Autonomy	Having the freedom to act on your own (more on this in Chapter 7).
Mastery	Having a challenge, wanting to get better and better at doing something that matters and that aligns with your talent.

As a manager, your task is to draw out mastery in the people you lead.

It would be a pity not to make use of the available potential and talent. Fostering employees' talents motivates, so go for it!

> *Strong leaders know their own strengths and know how to bring them out in their people.*

Universal strengths

One of the founders of positive psychology, Prof. Martin Seligman, has spent many years studying the positive qualities every person has. He has mainly worked on the applied science behind this so that you can actually put it to practical use.

Together with Christopher Peterson, he developed a list of 24 universal strengths to help you discover what gives you energy and doesn't require too much effort.

On average, every person has 5 to 7 characteristic strengths. You are capable of more, of course, but those activities cost you more energy than your personal top 5-7.

To give you an idea of what this might look like, below are three examples from that list.

Friendly and generous

You are generous and kind to others and you are never too busy to do someone a favor. You enjoy helping other people, even if you don't know them very well.

<u>Leadership</u>
You excel at leadership tasks, such as encouraging a group to get things done and maintaining harmony in the group by making everyone feel part of it.

<u>Honest, sincere, and authentic</u>
You are an honest person, not only because you speak the truth but also because you live a life that is sincere and authentic. You have your feet on the ground and do not put on a pretense—you are "real".

Exercise
You can discover your strengths by doing the free *"Via24 Character Strengths Test"* online.

Use this test for your team by having everyone take the test and printing their top five strengths on a card for the workplace. This way you get a good idea of people's individual strengths and it becomes easier to draw on them.

Recruitment based on talents
Fostering talent already starts at the recruitment stage. Traditional job postings are full of lists of what a candidate must know and what experience they must have to do the job.

Fortunately, "We hire on attitude" is an increasingly common credo; we hire people on the basis of their attitude (and not primarily on the basis of knowledge, because that is something you can easily learn).

Attitude describes the way a person responds to a situation. This is partly down to aptitude (Chapter 1), but you can imagine that people also respond more consciously or energetically in situations where they can draw on their strengths. So, when recruiting, consider what strengths you might still need in your team. When recruiting employees, pay attention to the combination of attitude and strengths based on the "VIA 24" test and you'll see that you become more successful at attracting the right people.

> *Don't go with the flow, be the flow*

Flow

You may already be familiar with the concept of "flow," which you often hear in radio and TV commercials. It is a theoretical concept proposed and named by Mihaly Csikszentmihalyi, who first used the term in 1975 and wrote the book "*Flow*".

Flow is a state of being that occurs when you are fully immersed in an activity. This can be work but also a leisure activity, for example when practicing sports.

When you are in a state of flow, you can get a lot more done. It gives you a boost of energy, is good for your health and contributes to happiness, including happiness at work.

Flow can be broken down into two axes, with the use and development of your skills on the horizontal axis and the extent to which you meet the challenge on the vertical axis.

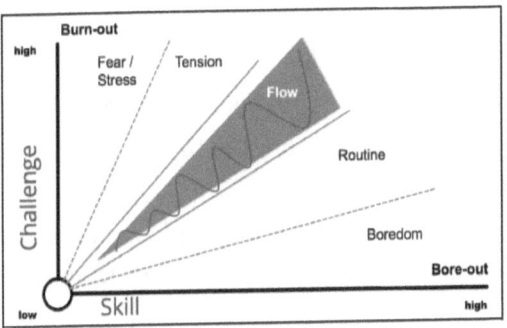

There are two extremes in this flow model, both of which can be detrimental to your health. Excessive challenge causes tension, stress and, ultimately, anxiety and burn-out. Not having or seeking enough challenge leads to monotonous work, tedium and ultimately, bore-out.

Experiencing flow regularly is not just good for you, it also encourages others to develop their skills. To experience flow, you need four things.

- **Direction** A clear purpose
- **Choice** You need to be able to make your own choices, for example the pace that's right for you

- **Challenge** Rather than settling for an easy fix, choose an activity that challenges your knowledge, skill, and experience
- **Feedback** Make sure you can see or feel your progress

Happiness at work

Positive psychology is also the foundation for happiness at work—a topic that is increasingly gaining ground in organizations, particularly because of its energizing effect on employees and the organization. It has many positive effects, such as lower absenteeism and lower staff turnover.

My first introduction to happiness at work was in 2017, when I left Rabobank because I was no longer happy. In my quest for happiness, I discovered that it is a very personal process and that it is difficult to pin down.

But at the same time it is, in essence, amazingly simple. One definition of happiness at work I came across is by Alexander Kjerulf, "*a feeling of happiness you experience at work*". In the current pandemic times, with many people working from home, you could say it is "a feeling of happiness you experience *while* working".

The great thing is that happiness at work often manifests itself into two factors: good results and your relationships with co-workers, customers, suppliers and so on.

Exercise

You can test this by thinking back to a pleasurable moment at work, be it yesterday, last week or five years ago. A time that made you happy and that you still remember with a smile.

Now ask yourself whether this experience matches either the "results" or the "relationships" aspect of happiness at work. There's a high chance the answer is "yes" to one or both aspects.

And good to know: Happiness at work is nurtured by the following factors.

- **Engagement**: You use your strengths in your work, you have room to develop and you experience being so fully immersed in an activity that you lose sense of time and place. In other words, being in a state of flow.

- **Purpose**: your work has added value; you are doing something meaningful. You may also feel it is important to make the world a better place through your work.

- **Positive emotions**: experiencing emotions such as joy, gratitude, inspiration and hope at work is often the most visible aspect of happiness at work.

Of these, "engagement" is the most important for fostering talent. For many employees, being engaged at work is the most important factor for long-term job happiness.

Chapter 7
Give people freedom

"Give people complete freedom" is one of the most famous quotes by Ricardo Semler, a Brazilian entrepreneur known for his 1993 book *"Semco Style"*.

He argues that you should get rid of all nonsensical rules and minimize bureaucracy. The company has no organization chart, meetings are voluntary, every employee has a say and chooses their own working hours, salary, and supervisor.

Self-management
There are also examples of leaders who have adopted this approach in the Netherlands, including Michiel Goemans, owner of eight Kinki Kappers hair salons throughout the country.

Taking inspiration from Semler, he "resigned" as boss and introduced "self-management". Accustomed to the strict hierarchical nature of the hairdressing profession, in 2014 he decided to run the business together with his employees.

The goal was to "work together to make this the world's happiest workplace, where our customers love to come".

Employees get a lot of freedom to come up with ideas, they know who is good at what and they take care of the planning themselves. So, they are in control of their own work and schedules rather than being constantly monitored by the boss.

Employees are visibly energized and are encouraged to use their talents and learn new things and they are generally happier.

"Get rid of all managers"
Self-management is about giving people trust and the freedom to make decisions themselves. Unfortunately, self-management has become synonymous with "get rid of all managers" and I see companies purging management layers without taking other actions. And that's a pity, because with self-management more people are taking the lead on things and this requires attention.

The main challenge in implementing self-management is deciding what you can let go of. Letting go is not easy for a lot of people, so let's see what can help!

Cultivating autonomy
In Chapter 6, I mentioned Dan Pink's research on intrinsic motivation with "Autonomy, having the freedom to act on your own", as one of three essential elements.

It is quite a lot to ask of a manager to let go and in practice it can be quite difficult. As a manager, you quickly resort to taking control and getting back into the driver's seat, especially when things get tricky.

Avoid giving too many instructions and wanting to be in control of everything yourself

Cultivating autonomy within your organization is a long-term strategy, and there are three things that can help you do that.

Situational leadership

Although you may think that situational leadership is old-fashioned, as you'll see, it is still highly relevant!

In the late 1960s, Ken Blanchard and Paul Hersey developed a model based on the premise that there is no single leadership style that works anytime, anywhere; the effectiveness of a particular style varies from one situation to another.

In other words, as a manager, you have to adapt to the person you are managing and look at the task and need at hand.

The model distinguishes four phases in employee development (and I can reveal that phases 3 and 4 have a lot in common with cultivating autonomy).

In brief, the four phases are:

Phase	Name	Style	Actions by the manager
1	Enthusiastic beginner	Instruction	A lot of task-oriented and practical guidance, showing them how to do it, giving tips, making action plans, and letting employee try things out

Phase	Name	Style	Actions by the manager
2	Learner with disillusionment	Super-vision	Asking employees questions, involving them, steering them in the right direction and, above all, encouraging them and giving them attention
3	Cautious employee	Coaching	Again, paying attention and especially listening, asking questions and following up, encouraging, and giving feedback. Encouraging employees to take personal responsibility
4	Self-managing employee	Delegation	Giving people freedom and their own responsibility, keeping them connected and above all showing them appreciation

So, this model is still relevant. Often I see managers resort to styles 1 and 2 in times of stress and uncertainty. These styles are primarily task-driven and give people less freedom.

Studies have shown that on average, only 15% of employees within a specific area of responsibility are self-managing employees (style 4). However, 83% of employees receive this style 4 leadership from their manager.

The result is that people are left to cope on their own and do not receive any attention, which has a negative impact on motivation, commitment, and people's happiness at work.

So, it is important that you accurately assess which leadership style suits a particular employee and then adjust your behavior accordingly.

It takes two to tango, meaningful conversations

Learn how to delegate: use GROW

Another essential ingredient for cultivating autonomy is allowing people to develop their skills so that they can perform tasks more independently.

This especially includes tasks that managers believe they can do "best" themselves (Style 4 of situational leadership is called "Delegation" for a good reason).

Many managers fall into the trap of wanting to come up with a solution as quickly as possible. And that's not how people learn things themselves.

You can prevent this by applying the GROW model—a conversation technique that helps you, when you are having conversations with the people you manage based on the other person's capacities and qualities.

Goal	Setting short-term and long-term goals
Reality	Evaluating the current situation
Options	Discussing options and alternatives
Way-forward	Who should do what and when?

The GROW model helps to break down a conversation with employees into individual steps. To truly get a conversation going, the emphasis is on Step 1 (Goal) and Step 2 (Reality), followed by a discussion of possible solutions in Step 3 (Options) and choices in Step 4.

If you do an online search for "GROW questions" you'll find a comprehensive range of questions for each step.

<u>Clear frameworks, freedom, and trust</u>
A third aspect of cultivating autonomy is setting clear frameworks and instilling trust.

I mentioned these frameworks earlier when discussing inspiration—as a leader, your aim is to inspire people with your story.

You communicate the mission, vision and strategy of the organization and create the framework to achieve this.

A case in point is Southwest Airlines with **"Live the Southwest Way"**. This American airline made headlines with a YouTube video of steward David Holmes giving—or better rapping—the safety instructions to passengers. What's special about this, you may ask?

Southwest has a rock-solid framework for their strategy and gives employees freedom and trust.

It encourages employees to live "The Southwest Way".

Elements of this strategy are:

- A Warrior Spirit (working hard, wanting to be the best, being courageous!)
- A Servant's Heart (others first, be of service!)
- A Fun-LUVing Attitude (be a team player, have fun!)

At Southwest, management truly gives employees the freedom to live the Southwest Way. Besides David's rap there are hundreds more videos on YouTube of Southwest employees having fun and entertaining passengers. From opera singers to all passengers on a plane getting a snorkel because of Southwest's first flight to the Caribbean.

Southwest's strength lies in the creative talents of its employees and the freedom they get from management. What is your strategy and how much freedom do you give to the people you lead to put it into practice?

> *Sometimes you win, sometimes you learn*

Learning from mistakes
Finally, a fantastic way to truly give people freedom—allowing mistakes (or boldly said fuck-ups). Many companies say, "you're allowed to make mistakes," but in practice it remains quite tricky. Often this means "you're allowed to make mistakes, but not too many".

A growing number of organizations have embraced making mistakes as part of their culture. A famous example is the Ben & Jerry's Flavor Graveyard in Vermont, USA. Next to the company's headquarters is a cemetery with tombstones of flavors that weren't successful. Useful as a reference for new taste developers and it's now also a tourist attraction.

Another example is from House of Performance, a Dutch consulting company where making mistakes is a must for a learning organization. It allows people to learn and dare to make mistakes. Employees (including managers) regularly present their mistakes to each other over Friday afternoon drinks and host the "Fuck-up of the Week" election.

Chapter 8
Never stop learning

> *"Once you stop learning, you start dying"*
> Albert Einstein

Chances are that as a manager, you can devote more time to your own work while giving your people the right kind of attention, especially after applying the tips I have given you so far.

In this chapter, I therefore focus on continuing to develop your own leadership qualities, for which there are several different approaches.

Blind spots
In Chapter 1, I described how you can ask for feedback on how you are doing with leading others. While feedback often has a negative connotation, it is a simple and highly effective way to continue to learn. So, make this a regular part of the conversations you have in your organization.

As a manager, you don't often get feedback so the more you ask for it yourself and take it seriously, the more you build a relationship of trust and continue to learn.

> *Feedback helps you overcome your blind spots*

The Johari window (designed by Joseph Luft and Harrington Ingham) gives insight into the view of others in combination with your own views on your behavior. Feedback can then help you to discover your blind spots.

So let's check-out the window:

	Known to you	Not known to you
Known to others	Open	**Blind spot**
Not known to others	Hidden	Not known

Blind spots can be very annoying and while people generally tend to talk about them, they usually don't tell you what yours are. Often this is an automatic and unproductive behavior of yours that others notice, without you being aware of it.

In her book *"Fearless Leadership,"* Loretta Melandro describes the ten most common blind-spot behaviors managers show.

Which do you recognize in yourself? And in others?

1. Going it alone
2. Being insensitive to your impact on others
3. Having an "I know" attitude
4. Avoiding difficult conversations
5. Blaming others or circumstances
6. Treating commitments casually
7. Conspiring against others
8. Withholding emotional commitment
9. Not taking a stand
10. Tolerating "good enough"

So, as you can see, it is important to ask for feedback, including about your blind spots.

I have seen sessions organized for teams to speak openly about a manager's blind spots in the absence of that manager.

Afterward, the manager joined the session, and the blind spots were discussed. Talk about daunting!

This allows organizations to make huge improvements and managers to truly develop their leadership skills, based on trust and on the input of employees.

Would you dare to do this? You should!

Feed-forward
The Johari window, which originated in 1955, is still extremely useful. Recent publications have focused on the feed-forward method, which is mainly future-oriented.

With the feed-forward approach, you take control of your development and ask co-workers to help you in this process.

A feed-forward conversation therefore broadens your options as a manager. Because you are the one asking for and (hopefully) wanting to hear feed-forward, the chance that you'll actually do something with it is much higher.

Exercise:
How does it work?

Step 1: Make sure you have a clear goal and know which aspects you want to develop.
Step 2: Tell this to the co-worker (or co-workers) with whom you are having the conversation.
Step 3: Then ask for advice that can help you achieve your goal.
(As this is future-oriented, you don't have to talk about what isn't going well).
Step 4: Listen carefully, do not engage in debate, and say, "thank you".
Step 5: After this conversation, you can put the advice you received into practice and then ask the people you spoke to whether they can see any effects or change. That way you maintain the connection and make them part of your development.

Change happens in steps

Real change in three steps

Change... Countless books have been written about it, and that's logical, for change is extremely difficult. It is a known fact that most attempts to bring about change fail, especially when it comes to behavioral change.

I'm sure you recognize this; you make resolutions to do things differently, for example after getting feedback, but quickly relapse into your old patterns.

Even after training sessions and courses (and maybe even after reading this book), the new insights soon fade away as you again become buried in daily life.

But you can do something about this!

In his book *"The Ladder,"* Ben Tiggelaar describes a change method based on three steps: goal, visible behavior, and support.

<u>Step 1, determine your goal</u>
First you determine the goal you want to achieve. As you develop your leadership skills, you often end up describing something you would like to be able to do more—or less. In terms of how your brain processes suggestions, this method works best when you formulate it positively.

Examples are:
- I want to pay more attention to my people.
- I want to delegate more by tapping into other people's qualities.
- I want to make asking for feedback a standard feature of my leadership toolbox.

Make sure you choose one goal at a time!

<u>Step 2, describe your desired behavior</u>
The next step is to come up with types of behavior you need to achieve your goal and to choose the one that will have the most impact.

It is important to describe the behavior in specific terms; "visible behavior" you can demonstrate it and others can see and emulate it.

Examples of this type of behavior:

- I ask at least three open questions in conversations with my people.
- I put aside at least half an hour a day in my calendar to walk around the department or call someone unexpected.
- I engage in at least three conversations each month based on the exercise of asking for feedback.

<u>Step 3, organize your support and resources</u>
Now you've clarified your goal and specific visible behavior, but you're not there yet.

Change is rarely something you can do on your own, so it is helpful to identify and seek support. Describe which techniques you can use to support your new behavior.

As a rule of thumb, it's best to choose three support techniques.

There are three drivers of behavioral change—your abilities (can I do this?), your motivation (do I want this?), and the environment (can I do it here?).

Here are a few examples of support:

- Follow a coaching leadership training course (capacity.
- Set up your own monitoring system, such as putting one marble in a jar on your desk for every feedback conversation you've had (motivation).
- Share your intention with your team and other co-workers and ask for their support (environment).

Learning new behaviors takes time, so plan for three to six months to learn the new behaviors and reach your goal. After that, you can start with a new goal. In the meantime, if you have mastered the new behavior but have not yet reached your goal, you can choose additional new behaviors to work on.

Good luck!

Chapter 9

Adopt a healthy lifestyle

A healthy lifestyle? I'm far too busy ...

It's like we're back to Chapter 2 right.. Your health affects everything in your life, yet I see signs everywhere that are not encouraging. Take, for instance, the Gallup studies:

- 23% of American workers said they felt burned out more often than not;
- just 33% of American workers are engaged by their jobs, 52% say they're "just showing up";
- and so on.

These statistics are not unique to the U.S.; you find the same pattern in many countries around the world.

I'd therefore like to take some time to talk about a healthy lifestyle and I'll break this down into vital leadership, healthy mental living (mindset) and healthy physical living (exercise, sleep, and nutrition).

Vital leadership
As a leader, this is especially important. Naturally, you are responsible for your own health and as a leader you also have a duty to set an example for others.

Your role as a leader is extremely important in creating a vital work environment. As a vital leader, you are not afraid to ask questions about health, lifestyle, and happiness, and thus set a good example yourself.

I call it vital leadership, and it is about:

- your own healthy living;
- the example this sets for others, and
- having a plan to promote healthy living within your organization/team.

A great example of an organization that actively promotes healthy living is Tony Chocoloney, a Dutch confectionery company that produces and sells chocolate.

Every year, everyone at the company can buy a pair of athletic shoes, walking sticks or another sports item from the sports bonus.

They also have a "maintain a good weight" bonus and a "don't smoke" bonus, which encourage a healthy lifestyle with a token amount of sixty dollars. It is based on trust, so no need to use scales.

Optimists are healthier and live longer

Mental healthy living
You spend a lot of your time working. The question is, how do you mentally process and handle it?

We can identify two mindsets for this:

Fixed: You believe your abilities are fixed and you avoid challenges.

Growth: You believe you can develop your abilities and are focused on solutions and opportunities. Now you might say "I have a growth mindset," because of course you believe in developing your abilities.

But in practice I see that this is quite an art (think back to the section on change in the previous chapter) and we seem to remain static in many areas.

So, it is not just about having a growth mindset but more importantly, actually activating it.

The question is, how do you do that? And the answer is...

Become an optimist!
Long-running research by Harvard University shows that optimists are healthier and live longer. While optimism is certainly a part of one's disposition, what has become clear is that the glass is half full if you make the conscious decision to see it as half full and keep doing that.

So, optimism can be learned. In his book *"Become an Optimist"* Leo Bormans shares the following tips:

1. <u>Reframe your setbacks</u>
   What appears to be a disaster can lead to new opportunities. Use your resilience to create a new framework of the existing situation. It is not just about positivity and always wanting to feel happy.

Life is full of adversity and the art is to be able to deal with this wisely. Often adversity, such as being laid off, also provides people with new opportunities.

2. <u>Pay attention to what makes you feel good</u>
   Seek out things that make you feel good. Is it your friends? Is it reading a book, playing sports, meditating? Hold on to the feeling and invoke it when you need it.

3. <u>Have a good conversation</u>
   This is one way for you to genuinely pay attention to your people. It can often lead to something beautiful and will nurture your confidence and optimism. Of course, you can also have a good conversation with a friend or family member, for example.

Exercise:
You can continue to develop positive feelings by writing down three things you are grateful for. Do this every day for at least three weeks (preferably a little longer). Also write down what made you mention this specific event.

This is an excellent form of optimism training for your brain, which normally pays attention to things that are not going well or that pose a threat.

Studies show that this exercise actually made participants happier and less stressed.

> *Staying positive in a negative situation is not being naive but being a leader.*

From DIP to TIP

Did you know that for many people, complaining co-workers are the biggest reason for having a bad day? Complaining is like dirty fuel for your brain and your health.

What about you—what do you do in the face of adversity?

As a manager, you often find yourself in difficult situations. Regulators with new rules, a boss who unexpectedly wants something from you, employees who don't do what you want them to do, and so on.

In such situations, it is important to stay positive and take the initiative.

Stephen Covey has written a lot about this and one of his most well-known models is "Circle of Influence and Circle of Concern".

His advice is to be proactive and focus your energy on things that are in your circle of influence and expand it: in other words, Think in Possibilities! (TIP).

The Circle of Concern is sometimes called the "Circle of Complaint".

An unpleasant situation arises, we resent it, judge it, feel powerless, criticize it, rebel against it, and complain to others. In short, Dwelling In Problems (DIP).

We all complain from time to time, and there is something positive about that too, because it is how we express our commitment and concerns. As a manager you can complain when things don't go well, but keep it short and make sure you don't set a bad example where your complaining becomes an excuse for others to do the same.

As a manager, keep an eye on when others complain. Rather than avoiding it, pay attention, ask what the matter is and help them find ways to resolve the issue.

You always have a choice! You can go from Dwelling In Problems to Think In Possibilities, so from DIP to TIP. In doing so, you demonstrate leadership.

Healthy lifestyle

<u>Moving</u>

We sit far too much—on average, we spend seven hours a day sitting.

The top two causes of work-related complaints are poor sitting posture and sitting for too long without breaks.

This is bad for your health, but what can you do about it?

- Introduce variety into your work: take short breaks, hold standing meetings, get an exercise/sitting ball...
- Always take the stairs.
- Go for a walk at lunch or during conversations with your co-workers.
- Do push-ups in between work tasks.
- Why not try team-planking for two minutes three times a day? This is also an excellent bonding activity!
- Pacing while talking on the phone is a great idea.
- You can also take part in sports activities, either alone or with your co-workers.

Extra Tip
Hospitals are, of course, places where it's all about improving health. I have been to several hospitals where the elevators have texts like "Taking the stairs keeps your joints flexible" and "Taking the stairs more often improves your fitness".

Another company regularly drops twenty-euro bills in the stairwell at random moments, which results in a noticeable reduction in the use of the elevators.

Sleep

A good night's rest prolongs life and we need 7 hours of sleep a night on average! Matthew Walker, a researcher who specializes in the power of sleep, showed that after just one night of sleeping fewer than 7 hours, all kinds of harmful effects occur in the brain and the rest of your body.

What can you do?

- Make sure you get about 7 hours of sleep a day; not too much and not too little.
- Avoid using digital devices just before you go to sleep, so switch off your smartphone on time (say at least 30-60 minutes) and read a book or take some time to meditate or reflect on the day.

Nutrition

And finally, a quick reminder of the importance of nutrition for a healthy life. Good nutrition is essential for our existence and health, and yet many people do not pay enough attention to it.

Only 25% of people meet the guidelines for good nutrition. What about you? Do you set a good example?

Take a look at your eating habits and if you want to make a change for the better, check out the book *"GUT, The Inside Story of our Body's Most Underrated Organ"* by Giulia Enders, who describes how your gut is an energy source for your brain.

Chapter 10

Don't forget to smile

> "A smile only lasts an instant,
> but the memory of it can be eternal"
> Raoul Follereau

The power of a smile

Children are extremely good at it; they laugh on average 7,7 times per hour and that's more than adults. We learn how to smile from an incredibly early age. In fact, you can even see a smile on a 3D ultrasound before birth. Isn't that cool!

Most of us seem to forget the ability to laugh as we grow older. Just walk around the office, the street, or a supermarket. You see little joy in people's faces and only 33% of people laugh more than twenty times a day, while 14% laughs even less than five times a day.

Yet we know that positive emotions are the most important and most recognizable source of happiness at work. A smile is a visible expression of joy and satisfaction.

Coffee vs. Laughter

Did you know that we consider laughter at work even more important than good coffee?

Insurance company Aevitae carried out studies showing that 87% of employees consider it important or especially important to laugh at work.

This is even higher than the desire for a good cup of coffee or tea (77%).

And it makes sense, because laughing makes the body produce the hormone dopamine (one of the happiness hormones).

A smile is contagious
And... a smile has an impact on others because we imitate what we see around us with our mirror neurons. When you smile, it has an effect on others.

Just smile at a co-worker in the elevator or the guy at the checkout counter of your supermarket. It almost always elicits a positive response!

Extra Tip
Be sure to check out Rituals' Happy Buddha ad on YouTube (Tram Man) or Coca Cola's in the Paris metro (Happiness starts with a smile).

You'll see that you naturally join in the laughter. These videos are also great as an energizer during a team meeting, for example.

Spend more time smiling than frowning

Find your smile!
Smile consciously and use your optimism and humor as a keystone for your leadership. Managers who regularly smile are appreciated more and also more successful.

Of course, there's not always a reason to smile—think of failed projects or reorganizations, for example.

These are difficult situations, but it is where you, as a manager, can make a difference by approaching them with a positive attitude. Look for opportunities and, above all, listen and pay attention to your people. This positive attitude often starts by relaxing and finding your inner smile!

Your body responds (because your muscle activity affects the brain), you become less tense and it lowers your stress. This allows you to make a difference, even (or especially) in difficult situations. Leading with a smile—it makes a difference, both in good and not so good times.

That's it folks!
And that's it folks, my stories and advice to help you develop your leadership skills and your impact on others.

I hope this book have helped you to discover that leadership really is your thing!

You lead because it suits you, it's fun to do, it feels good, makes you happy and even better: the people around you appreciate it.

Hopefully, you can already feel that smile on your face! ☺

"The shortest distance between two people is a smile"

Buddha

Checklist for leading with a smile	
1. Know thyself	
- Discover your Big Five personality type	
- What's your compass?	
- Ask for feedback	
2. Seek wisdom in silence	
- Avoid choice stress	
- Reflect	
- Meditate	
3. Do everything with intent and focus	
- Pomodoro technique	
- The 4 "A"s	
- Use all your senses	
4. Inspire and motivate	
- Begin with the Why	
- Spark and Flame	
- Three leadership hats	
- How do you motivate people?	
- The languages of appreciation	
5. Walk the talk	
- Authenticity	
- In practice	
- Exemplary behavior	
6. Encourage talent	
- Develop mastery	
- Universal strengths—VIA24	
- Talent-based recruitment	
- Flow	
- Happiness at work	
7. Give others freedom	
- Self-management, cultivating autonomy	
- Situational leadership	

Checklist for leading with a smile	
- Learn how to delegate, GROW	
- Clear frameworks, freedom, and trust	
- Learning from mistakes	
8. Never stop learning	
- Blinds spots	
- Feed-forward	
- Real change in three steps	
9. Adopt a healthy lifestyle	
- Vital leadership	
- Become an optimist	
- From DIP to HIP	
- Moving	
- Sleep	
- Nutrition	
10. Don't forget to smile	
- The power of a smile	
- It's contagious	
- Find your smile!	

Reference list

- *For Personality at Work*, Pierce J. Howard, National Book Network, 2000
- *Happiness at Work*, Onno Hamburger and Ad Bergsma, Boom Uitgevers Amsterdam, 2013
- *Top Five Regrets of the Dying*, Bronnie Ware, Hay House UK Ltd, 2019
- *Busy,* Tony Crabbe, Piatkus, 2015
- *How to Break Up with Your Phone,* Catherine Price, Ten Speed Press, 2018
- *"The Power of your Subconscious" Dutch: Het slimme onderbewuste*, Ap Dijksterhuis, Prometheus/Bert Bakker, 2015
- *Pomodoro Technique*, Francesco Cirillo, Maven Publishing, 2018
- *Start with Why*, Simon Sinek, Penguin Books Ltd, 2011
- *Inspire! What Great Leaders Do*, Lance Secretan, John Wiley & Sons Inc, 2004
- *The 5 Languages of Appreciation, Gary Chapman and Paul White, Northfield Publishing, 2019*
- *Drive*, Daniel Pink, Canongate Books Ltd, 2018
- *Authentic Happiness*, Martin Seligman, John Murray Press, 2017
- *Flow*, Mihaly Csikszentmihalyi, HarperCollins Publishers Inc, 2008
- *Semco Style*, Ricard Semler, Boekerij, 2010

- *Management of Organizational Behavior,* Paul Hersey, Pearson, 1996
- *Fearless Leadership*, Loretta Melandro, McGraw-Hill Education, 2009
- *"The Ladder", Dutch: De Ladder*, Ben Tiggelaar, Tyler Roland Press, 2018
- *"Become an Optimist", Dutch: Word Optimist,* Leo Bormans, Lannoo, 2016
- *GUT,* Giulia Enders, Greystone Books, 2018

www.ingramcontent.com/pod-product-compliance
Lightning Source LLC
Chambersburg PA
CBHW031444210526
45464CB00005B/2323